Under the Canopy
100 Poems That Reconnect the Father's Heart to Yours

For permission requests and inquiries, please contact Katelyn Gannon at katelynmgannon@gmail.com

The following Bible translations have been used in this book: English Standard Version, New American Standard Bible, New International Version, New King James Version, The Passion Translation, and the New Living Translation.

ISBN 979-8-218-54858-2

Graphic Designer: Adelita Mendez

Under the Canopy
Katelyn Gannon

Under the Canopy

This book is dedicated to -

My mom, who encouraged me to start

and

My husband, who encouraged me to finish.

CONTENTS

A Season of Gratitude

A Season of Grief

A Season of Grace

A Season of Growth

PREFACE

WHAT IS THIS BOOK ABOUT?

This book is an invitation to return to the Father and His presence by communing with Him daily. These poems were born out of a place of trust and reliance on Jesus through all seasons of my life. While collecting these poems, I've looked back on each one and can remember either the moment in which I wrote it or the moment when God spoke it to me.

He presents Himself uniquely to us in every season of our lives. I've known Jesus to be the provider in one season and a sustainer in another. I've known Him to be gentle at times and loud at other times. Whatever season you're in, you can experience God. Whether it's a season of rejoicing, mourning, waiting, or plowing; it's more about experiencing than enduring. He is the gift of goodness throughout.

WHO DOES THIS BOOK SERVE?

Anyone that longs to connect with Jesus in a deeper way. Anyone who's curious to hear what He has to say. Any lover of Jesus that desires to know Him more.

WHAT MAKES THIS BOOK SPECIAL?

This book has been a work in process for 7 years. This is a collection of writings from years of singleness, joblessness, motherlessness, purposelessness, a cross-country move, a global pandemic, etc. But there has been so much joy! I remember in one particular season of rest and waiting where the Holy Spirit whispered to my heart that "many can not afford to have a season like this." I didn't have to ask what He meant by this because I knew. He continued with -

"It's something that's desired by many, but unfortunately few receive.
It's a season that looks purposeless and seems fruitless.
It's uneventful and mysterious and not attractive to the public eye.
Many may pity you; but they do not envy you.

For those who are sucked into the mundane of living wish they had more minutes in my presence.
Many do not know what they're missing.
Take this time, these minutes in your day that are left to waste, to spend with me."

I had moved back home to live with my parents after college and had applied to countless jobs. I took frequent walks in this beautiful community garden across the street. It was quite large, hosting hundreds of plants, hostas, and flowers. It was on these walks with the Lord where I began to recognize His voice in my spirit very clearly and it came to me through poetry. He spoke to me in a new and creative way that was special to me. He desires to speak to each of us, but we tend to make the hearing part of the conversation complicated. I realized many do long to hear the Lord's voice but are not willing to make the sacrifice to spend time with Him and really know His voice. We all have choices in how we spend our time, yet God longs to spend it with His children. Don't miss what He wants to say.

HOW DO YOU INTEND FOR ONE TO READ THIS BOOK?

These poems are short, and the scriptures provided throughout serve as an encouragement for you to personally tap into what Jesus may be wanting to say to you. I suggest reading a poem a day and reading the scripture in multiple translations. I love looking into the different meanings of words and one translation may speak something totally new to you. When I felt there was some story or explanation to a poem, I wrote a mini devotion in hopes of further depth and understanding.

Enjoy these next 100 days of being reconnected to the Father's heart!

From the beginning
I have been pursuing you
My love has chased you down and
Sought you out

My love hasn't been hidden
And it's been under no constraint
Goodness will follow until the end
Come, and let me show you

A Season of Gratitude

The Stream

Attending to Your will
Lord, carry me like a stream
Where You lead, I'll follow
For You bring me joy complete

Wherever we go, wherever we flow
I know I'll never hunger and thirst
For all my needs are met by You
So carry me like a stream

The current carries Your goodness
And constantly pours out Your purity
Living waters reside in this stream
In it, everything can breathe

So like the water, carry me too
Endlessly and quietly
Forever
I'll live in You

"Anyone who believes in me may come and drink! For the Scriptures
declare, 'Rivers of living water will flow from his heart.'"
John 7:38 NLT

Who You Are

You speak to dry bones and they awake
You speak to desolate places and they flourish
You speak to the darkness and light is birthed

A carrier of truth, love, and power
You usher in life
That is who You are

You call us to walk with You
To invite You in
For that is who You are

Worries vanish in Your presence
You take my burdens upon Yourself because
That is who You are

Then he said to me, "Prophesy to these bones and say to them, 'Dry bones, hear the word of the Lord! This is what the Sovereign Lord says to these bones: I will make breath enter you, and you will come to life. I will attach tendons to you and make flesh come upon you and cover you with skin; I will put breath in you, and you will come to life. Then you will know that I am the Lord.'"
Ezekiel 37:4-6 NIV

Above It All

I'm humbled and in awe at the way
You respond to Your creation
You lean down from heaven to listen
to the prayers of the faithful and
the cries of the righteous

Your eyes are roaming earth to and fro
Your ears listening to the praises
of the ones You love
I'm humbled and in awe at the way
You respond to Your children

Some think You're distant and
aloof to what we feel
Unaware of what's happening in the world
But I know Your heart is breaking
and Your spirit is grieving at the rejection You receive

Humanity can be careless in what You've
given us dominion over
Only You are the true and righteous judge
One day You'll right the wrongs of all the suffering
Laughing at the plots of the wicked - You're above it all

"Because he inclined his ear to me, therefore I will call on him as long
as I live."
Psalm 116:2 ESV

A Time Such as This

For a time such as this You were sent to be born
An earthly king as a babe in human form
The hope and light of the world is heaven's gift
For every person who calls on Your name
There You shall dwell and live

For a time such as this You were sent to die
Rejected by those whom You loved, now they crucify
Sent to save a creation that was born by just one breath
We are an eternal continuum of Your 'Ruach'
There is now no separation when we find ourselves in You

"By the word of the Lord the heavens were made,
and by the breath of his mouth all their host."
Psalm 33:6 ESV

Faithful and True

Your name is faithful and true
There's purity in all that You do

You wear a robe dipped in blood
but it illuminates light

I follow behind You on a horse that is white
I follow behind You
my master
my friend
my bridegroom
my God
my one and only

Oh that You would deem me worthy to be in Your entry line
That You would call me to follow suit!

That You would give me a horse -
my very own horse!
One that is white and dazzling just as Yours

You're a good dad and a noble king
who only gives His children good things

I've always wanted to wear a crown
to live in a kingdom
to be loved by a prince
to wear a gown that sparkled with jewels adorned

Oh to be cherished by You and to be chosen into Your
priesthood
It's an eternal promise
One I've been fashioned into

Your name is faithful and true
You keep Your word and fulfill a lifetime
of "I Will" and "I AM"

"I saw heaven standing open and there before me was a white horse,
whose rider is called Faithful and True. With justice he judges and
wages war. His eyes are like blazing fire, and on his head are many
crowns. He has a name written on him that no one knows but he
himself. He is dressed in a robe dipped in blood, and his name is the
Word of God. The armies of heaven were following him, riding on
white horses and dressed in fine linen, white and clean. Coming out of
his mouth is a sharp sword with which to strike down the nations. "He
will rule them with an iron scepter." He treads the winepress of the
fury of the wrath of God Almighty. On his robe and on his thigh he
has this name written:

'KING OF KINGS AND LORD OF LORDS.'"
Revelation 19:6-11 NIV

Testify

This is my testimony -

My God came down from Heaven to Earth
to capture my heart in a way that only He could
He paid for an eternity of no sickness, sin, and grave

One drop of blood would've been enough
but He willingly gave it all as the spotless lamb
He kept His word and rose on the third day

From death to life so I could remain alive in Him
It's the greatest love story
and it's mine to tell

"Unlike those other high priests, he does not need to offer sacrifices
every day. They did this for their own sins first and then for the sins of
the people. But Jesus did this once for all when he offered himself as
the sacrifice for the people's sins."
Hebrews 7:27 NLT

The Father's Reward

It's so sweet to sing Your praise
To get locked in and hold Your gaze
Blessed are those pure in heart
For they will see You

It's so sweet to trust Your name
To know that You'll do what You say
Blessed are those who are persecuted
For theirs is the kingdom of heaven

It's so sweet to abide in Your grace
To know that it will all be okay
Blessed are those who give mercy
For they shall receive mercy just the same

It's so sweet to call on Your name
To know that we have Your full attention
Blessed are those who hunger and thirst
For righteousness for they will be satisfied

It's so sweet to have You as a friend
To know that you stick closer than a brother
Blessed are those who live in harmony
For they shall be called sons of God

In all these things I will rejoice
For my reward is not on earth
Nor do I strive for such attention in this matter
I hope to captivate the audience of just one
That is the reward of a proud Heavenly Father

Behold

Behold
Prepare to witness something great
Ready your ears to listen to heaven
Observe the miraculous with the eyes of your heart
Testify to wonder

Come and behold Him
Gaze upon your Savior's face
Take note of His beauty
His holiness
And worship in awe

Don't miss it
Don't rush it -
For this is a beholding moment

Then the angel said to them, "Do not be afraid, for behold, I bring you
good tidings of great joy which will be to all people"…
Luke 2:10 NKJV

Your Perspective

I lift my eyes to the skies
and into the heavens
to see from Your perspective

Though there's chaos; peace is hovering
Though there's destruction; truth is being spoken
Though there's anger; love is on display

So I lift my eyes to the skies
and into the heavens
With all that is within me, I declare
let Your will be done here on earth

"Your kingdom come.
Your will be done,
On earth as it is in heaven."
Matthew 6:10 NASB

Todah

Give thanks, receive joy
Give thanks, receive grace
Give thanks, receive peace
Give thanks, because God is good

"Rejoice always, pray without ceasing, in everything give thanks; for this
is the will of God in Christ Jesus for you."
1 Thessalonians 5:16-18 NKJV

Under the Sun

It's said that nothing new is born under the sun
All that was and is to come will be
All the creatures, the sky, the sea
So may we walk in wonder now of all that we can see

With nothing new to breed our curiosity
How do we walk in wonder?
We must revive our sight
To bring us fresh perspective

Inventions not yet discovered
Dreams not yet developed
We can create a new routine
To remove monotonous obstacles

So that we can continually walk in wonder
A fresh light must be given
Because nothing new will be born under the sun
There is enough beauty in the world to satisfy

"History merely repeats itself. It has all been done before. Nothing
under the sun is truly new."
Ecclesiastes 1:9 NLT

Reunion

By Your breath You formed man
Out of dust is where we began
In Your image You birthed
A son, a daughter, a friend

Out of nothing into something
It's sometimes too much to comprehend

Your heartbeat is for humanity
So humbly You came
You stopped at nothing
To create that connection again

On the cross You bridged the gap
To bring back what once was
A place filled with perfect peace
One day and forever with You, in harmony

"This is the promise which He Himself made to us: eternal life."
1 John 2:25 NASB

Humble Beginnings

Take delight in the small things
The sparks of hope I send your way
For one day all the small flickers
Will turn into a wonderful display

"Do not despise these small beginnings, for the LORD rejoices to see
the work begin, to see the plumb line in Zerubbabel's hand."
Zechariah 4:10 NLT

This I Believe

I still believe You're good
And I still believe You're just

I still believe in the power of the cross
I just want to say that I still believe

Even as the sun will rise
And the stars will shine
Is Your love
Oh Your amazing love for me

Even as the years go by
You'll always be by my side

Oh how I have a friend in my God

Don't let your heart become jaded with the grind of a new season.
Allow expectancy and thankfulness to take your heart places your mind
can't.

Live Free

How freeing it is to live life without a concrete plan
To trust all our days to someone and put them in His hands
To allow ourselves to feel delight and surprise
To walk in adventure
It's usually better than I've pictured

"In all your ways acknowledge him,
and he will make straight your paths."
Proverbs 3:6 ESV

Bless His Name

In the morning when I rise
I'll bless Your name
Make melody to You and sing Your praise
Utter back to You what You've already said

I'll speak from my heart
It's just You and I in the room
It's time to pour out my love on You
You're too worthy not to bless

Throughout my day I'll say Your name
To remind myself that You're close and You're near
To know that You take part in all the little tasks with me
While orchestrating in the heavenlies

In the evening when I rest
I'll bless Your name
Make melody to You and sing Your praise
Utter back to You what You've already said

You're making known to me the works of Your hands
By Your spirit, imparting Your plan
So I too can decree and declare that
Your Word may be done on this earth

I'll whisper Your faithfulness through the night
Dream of our friendship that I'll hold on tight
So that when I wake in the morning I can still retain
All of the ways You've blessed me just the same

"O Lord, in the morning you hear my voice"…
Psalm 5:3 ESV

The Potter's House

Today I went to the potter's house
Inside were shelves lined with an assortment of handmade
works of art
Each design so intricate, telling its own story
In front of me is a large wooden table with all sorts of tools
Discards of clay that have not yet been used

But You've not thrown the discards away
Perhaps they're just awaiting their time of significance
With a clump of clay in Your hands
I sit beside and eagerly await

Could You really make that into something beautiful?
Your eyes are determined with curiosity flickering
You're molding, shaping, and pressing it between Your
hands
Creating with such intent

I can tell this is one of Your favorite things to do
Making something unseen, unused, and undesirable into
something brand new
Now You've given it a purpose
I see You forming the handle and cupping its base
Perhaps it will hold some hot tea or fresh brewed coffee

You know me so well
You've made me a gift
You've given me a piece of Your work
You see me as such

cont.

I was sitting in church one morning when I saw an image of God, the potter, making something beautiful. I wrote what I saw and what came to my spirit. Afterwards, I met some friends for brunch and as we were walking we passed this pottery shop. Inside we went and there was a big wooden table in the center of the room with scraps of clay, and a lady in the front corner making pottery. I love how Jesus first spoke to me of how He views me, and then gave me a visual image shortly after. He sees each of us as His masterpiece. He made each of us carefully, thoughtfully, and with attention to detail. Not one of us are alike; we are an original.

Remain Grateful

I wish flowers lasted forever
I wish family would stay
I wish all pain would go away
I wish summer didn't fade

But that's a scary thing to wish

To wish something outside the will of God

His plan is good
His heart is kind
He is constantly changing old for new
Giving life back to the dead

So for that -
I am grateful

"Rejoice always, pray without ceasing, give thanks in all circumstances;
for this is the will of God in Christ Jesus for you."
1 Thessalonians 5:16-18

You Satisfy

Only You can pave a way through the dark
Only You can speak to my weary heart
Only You satisfy

I can search the world
Find home in a new place, new city
But only You satisfy

I can find meaning in friendship
Purpose in my work, even in the church
But only You satisfy

I can find comfort in earthly riches
Pleasure in tasteful foods
But only You satisfy

"Blessed [joyful, nourished by God's goodness] are those who hunger
and thirst for righteousness [those who actively seek right standing with
God], for they will be [completely] satisfied."
Matthew 5:6 AMP

My Helper

In all the changing and shifting
You're more steady than ever
An anchor that holds me
One I've never been more sure of

I feel vulnerable and I feel helpless
Except for this undenied grace that's present
An inner strength offered by Your spirit
It's persistent and consistent

Thank You for holding me
Thank You for walking with me
When I call upon Your help
You're there in a moment

"The steadfast love of the Lord never ceases;
his mercies never come to an end"…
Lamentations 3:22 ESV

The Anthem Song

He who has no end
let your glory fall on this land

Awake and arise my soul
to see your plan unfold

Jesus, You have no end

This is our anthem song
Church - come awake
Dry Bones - come alive
Lord speak to the empty spaces
and we'll see them revived

Fear has no place
Joy is our strength
With one voice we cry
Jesus be glorified

If life and death reside in the tongue
then may my words ring in a sound of hope
and carry a song of revival
For in the blood of the Lamb lives victory

A song written during the Covid-19 pandemic.

Standing on a Promise

I begged for a word to hold onto
Now I've seen Your goodness come through
Where fear once caused doubt
Your love won out
I'm standing on a promise fulfilled
Oh yes
I'm standing a promise fulfilled

"The Lord is not slow in keeping his promise, as some understand
slowness. Instead he is patient with you, not wanting anyone to perish,
but everyone to come to repentance."
2 Peter 3:9 NIV

Goodness and Mercy

When I was in my wandering and when I was in my doubt
goodness and mercy were there

When I was questioning Your plan for me and losing hope
goodness and mercy were there

When I was finding love and discovering the new
goodness and mercy were there

When I was saying goodbye to a place I thought I'd plant
roots
goodness and mercy were there

When I was reciting vows and exchanging wedding rings
goodness and mercy were there

I think I've found the secret -

That when I dwell with You
whether I usher words of thanks, deep cries of pain, or love
songs to You
goodness are mercy are there
because You're there too

"Surely goodness and mercy shall follow me all the days of my life, and
I shall dwell in the house of the LORD forever."
Psalm 23:6 ESV

A Call to Awaken Faith

My faith for marriage jumped in 2023
I woke up on January 1st with great expectancy

I felt this surge of faith where
you know that *you know* that you know
it's going to happen, that kind of feeling

Most of the time faith is subtle
and more of a quiet assurance
But other times faith feels big -
like a bold declaratory roar!

In times of doubt I found myself
asking the Lord to increase my faith once more

I look at my husband and stand assured
that God wrote this great love story
But it took my permission
my willingness
and my faith

A sacrifice to not settle on either end -
God knew we would be better as one
and could do much for His Kingdom

Out of His love and matchless creativity
He chose to connect us in the most unique way
Through a missionary couple from Singapore
a lasting impression to stay

cont.

What is something in your life that needs faith to awaken it? I ask that Jesus would increase your faith for it! That you would live in His joy by His Spirit. That in the waiting, you would strengthen yourself in His delight and truth. And that would feel His all consuming love nearer, still nearer.

A Season of Grief

Even Now

You are faithful
even when I'm not
You are stable
even when I'm not

I may sway and I may wander
But You, Oh God, will never leave
I may doubt and I might fear
But You, Oh God, don't worry for a second
about my insecure ways!

You remind me to trust You
When have You failed me?
You remind me of Your vast love
and I come into perfect peace

You surround me even now
in the thick of sadness and grief
With supernatural strength and comfort
Your right hand is upholding me

"For I the Lord do not change; therefore you, O children of Jacob, are
not consumed."
Malachi 3:6 ESV

Steady Me

You steady me like the sun
Firm in my position
Sure of my purpose
Fully obedient to Your will

Despair will not hold me down
Hope will be my anchor
Your word, I will feast
Your face, I will seek

"So He humbled you, allowed you to hunger, and fed you with manna
which you did not know nor did your fathers know, that He might
make you know that man shall not live by bread alone; but man lives by
every *word* that proceeds from the mouth of the Lord."
Deuteronomy 8:3 NKJV

Reconciliation

I'm trading the old for new
Lord, reconcile my heart to You
Clear away the misconceptions
and bridge the gaps I've made

Remove my heart of stone
and give me one of flesh
Not of my own likeness
but made in the image of You

With forgiveness in the heart
hate will no longer stand
I'm dying to my desires
to live a righteous life in You

If life and death reside in the tongue
then may my words ring in a sound of hope
and carry a song of revival
For in the blood of the Lamb lies victory

"My old self has been crucified with Christ. It is no longer I who live,
but Christ lives in me. So I live in this earthly body by trusting in the
Son of God, who loved me and gave himself for me."
Galatians 2:20 NLT

Locked Eyes

In hard times when I'm tempted to hide
I will look up and catch Your gaze
Transfixed on heaven and warmed by Your embrace
You've given me eyes to see Your face

Your light lifts the shadow
And everything is made clear
It's all made easy in Your presence
You've given me ears to hear Your word

Fresh wonder leads the way
Through the clouds and to Your gates
Sea glass and cherubim and flowers made of ruby
You've given me imagination to understand Your ways

"So all of us who have had that veil removed can see and reflect the
glory of the Lord. And the Lord—who is the Spirit—makes us more
and more like him as we are changed into his glorious image."
2 Corinthians 3:18 NLT

The Land in Between

The land in between seems unloving at first
It's the place of "not anymore" but "not yet"
Here is where
I blame
I shame
I complain
Am I forgotten?

I read of the Israelites and think no way could that be me
I'm not that blind to my reality
But then -
I blame
I shame
I complain
Am I forgotten?

All the while forgetting God's faithfulness
All the while not seeing what He's doing now

I don't want to miss the pruning
The shaping
The chipping
The refining

I'm done losing my mind
Trying to reckon with the ways of God

So perhaps it's here in the land in between
Where Your love meets my waiting with soft beckoning
Inviting me to be a part of the process

Hold On

I'm still holding onto hope
It's a daily choice I make
but sometimes I wonder -
how much more can I take?

I'm still holding onto a promise
that He keeps by design
It's His nature
and no one can change His mind

I'm still holding onto peace
It's steady like a stream
and it doesn't need much help from me
So I'll let go and let myself flow

I'm still holding onto a love story
where a moment of wonder
turns into a tangible thing
It's grander and more wild than I know

I'm still holding onto You
because you're faithful in everything you do
I see and know in part
but I know You're worthy to hold my heart

…"so that by two unchangeable things, in which it is impossible for
God to lie, we who have fled for refuge might have strong
encouragement to hold fast to the hope set before us."
Hebrews 6:18 ESV

A Cry for Wonder

Come move upon my limitations
And stretch all of my expectations
You are a God who does great things
You are a God who does great things

Come teach me wisdom in the hidden
Secrets that I have yet to know
Blow through all my fears and locked up spaces
Until I'm back at home with You

You're a teacher of truth
Yet You don't reject my shout
There is still freedom and beauty
In a sacrifice that's shattered

I wrote this poem in a difficult season where I was longing to be "wow'd" by God. I felt unsatisfied with where I was in life and I longed to see Him move powerfully. I was longing for a change. This was the honest prayer of my heart, to see Him move upon my limitations and stretch all expectations. I was asking God to help me to dream bigger and to show me something amazing! Because I know He does great things, I needed Him to raise my faith.

Hope Defined

It takes strength to hope again
To dream in spite of disappointment
To not slumber and stay there

Almost like there needs to be something
one can grasp when all else falls through the cracks

What is that thing?

Hope

"May the God of hope fill you with all joy and peace in believing, so
that by the power of the Holy Spirit you may abound in hope."
Romans 15:13 ESV

Lean In

In your waiting, God is working
He is not bound by time as you are
He isn't moved by the waves as you are

In your hurting, God sees you
He isn't absent
His peace will carry you unlike anything you've felt

You must dig deeper in this season
You must choose joy

Hope will be with you every step you take
As you daily proclaim victory
In Jesus name

Consider it nothing but joy, my brothers and sisters, whenever you fall
into various trials. Be assured that the testing of your faith [through
experience] produces endurance [leading to spiritual maturity, and inner
peace]. And let endurance have its perfect result *and* do a thorough
work, so that you may be perfect and completely developed [in your
faith], lacking in nothing.
James 1:2-4 AMP

Prodigal

Return to my love
Return to my heart
Return to the moment you first heard my voice

Return to the day you were first captured by my presence
Return to me
As nothing was or is before me

Find me again and you'll find light
Find me again and you'll find yourself
Find me again and you'll find your reason for living

I'm not hard to find
I'm not fond of hiding
Come seek and come knock
And out I will come

"Even now," says the Lord,
"Turn *and* come to Me with all your heart [in genuine repentance],
With fasting and weeping and mourning [until every barrier is removed
and the broken fellowship is restored]"…
Joel 2:12 AMP

The Ugly Flesh

It's not about me
That's what I tell myself
"I'm thinking about you"
Is what I hear my mouth speak
Do I believe it?
I want to

It's not about me
Yes, I know
How can I help you?
What can I do for you?
But do I dare ask those questions?
I want to

It's not about me
I'm daydreaming again
What are your dreams?
What do you think about?
These things I want to know
If I only stopped thinking of me

In the context of serving one, I've found myself asking these questions.
I want to believe what I speak. I want my heart to be kind and pure
24.7. I want to stop for the one, to focus, to love, and to hit pause on
my selfish ways. It's humbling and even aggravating at times how stuck
we can be on ourselves. We desire to be *good*, but it's only by the Holy
Spirit that we are ever truly *good*. Holy Spirit, help us today to walk in
Your ways. To let go of distractions. To let go of things that don't
matter. And to see the one in front of us as Jesus does.

My Prayer

In the present, be my God
In the still, be my God
In the here and now, be my God
In the valley, be my God
In the fire, be my God
In the drought, be my God

Walk by me
Surround me
Lead me
Stand by me
Fight for me
Cover me
Carry me

For you sustain and you fulfill
You will not leave me alone
You won't desert me, for you Lord have made your home
within my heart
You entrust your kingdoms to me
You've made me into the image of you
You've made me a light for you

For where can I go that you don't see?
For where will I go that you won't follow?

You in me, and I with you, I won't stray for whatever
You in me, and I with you, nothing will separate
You in me, and I with you, Jesus forever

A Renewed Mind; A Renewed Life

Everything you're looking at
I have made
This breeze is my very breath
Surely I will take care of you

When you're feeling weak and
in need of strength
Have you renewed your mind with my spirit?
Refreshed your soul with my words?

What if the thing you're holding out for
is the thing I have you destined for?

I'll make knowing Your voice a practice
Calling on You daily an exercise
Renewing my mind a habit
So I know You intimately
My life - Your worship

"But the hour is coming, and is now here, when the true worshipers
will worship the Father in spirit and truth, for the Father is seeking such
people to worship him."
John 4:23 ESV

Light

The light can only brighten the darkness
The night does not overtake the day
But the sun willingly sets so we can have rest
and experience peace
The light can only brighten the darkness

"The light shines in the darkness, and the darkness has not overcome
it."
John 1:5 ESV

Feast

You guide my steps
You light up my path when I need to see it
And when I don't -
give me faith to trust

Things that are extraordinary will become ordinary
as I feast on heavenly realities
With hope as my guarantee
and wonder as the key

There is fresh bread each day
to hunger after
There is comfort inside of the fire
with you by my side

"Blessed is the one who trusts in the LORD, who does not look to the
proud, to those who turn aside to false gods."
Psalm 40:4 NIV

Abundant Living

In your waiting I see you
In your waiting I hold you

Hold steadfast to my promises
I will remind you...
again...
because I love you

I promise you a love so great
A life so abundant in me
that nothing will compare to what I offer
Nothing in this whole world will compare
Do you understand?
Do you comprehend?

Nothing compares to the love I have for you!!!
Come to me
You're not alone
For I have heard you

You're free to sing
Dance
Laugh!

Live unto whom I've called you to be
Who I've destined you to be
The enemy cannot steal your joy anymore

Laugh
Sing of your praises unto me
There's freedom in my presence

cont.

Go on - ask me your questions
Voice your concerns
Tell me your opinions

This was a word I received from the Lord many years ago. He was
inviting me to come into abundant living! It's my choice. He desires
close union with us all, but we must want it.
The God of the universe wants to commune *with you* today.

I Won't Turn

Do not harden your heart to His love
His people or even His strange ways of doing
A hardened heart keeps you from His promises
A hardened heart keeps you from seeing His face
A hardened heart keeps you from understanding His ways

A lofty mind may keep you elevated
but your spirit will remain crushed

Sin keeps you unresponsive to God -
Who He is as a father and friend
Who He is as a Savior and brother

So in my days of testing, I will choose You
In my days of mourning, I will choose You
In my days of trials, I will choose You

I give You permission to search my heart daily
To keep my heart soft and my words tender and sweet
Today is all I have
If I hear Your voice, I won't turn

Therefore, as the Holy Spirit says,
"Today, if you hear his voice, do not harden your hearts as in the
rebellion, on the day of testing in the wilderness, where your fathers
put me to the test and saw my works for forty years."
Hebrews 3:7-9 ESV

Brighter

I'm lost at sea
Trying to find a little piece of land
A little piece of security so I can stand

The horizon seems distant
It feels distant
Oh I can't see

But this light of Yours inside can't be contained
I feel it illuminate through all the pain

Only Your light can brighten the darkness
There's no shadow that can hide it
Because even in the secret
I can find it
It's Your light that brightens the darkness

Jesus, Your love is brighter
it's grander
than the waves

Jesus, Your love is greater
so much stronger
than anything I face

"Then Jesus again spoke to them, saying, "I am the Light of the world;
the one who follows Me will not walk in the darkness, but will have the
Light of life."
John 8:12 NASB

Faith Explained

A perfect faith -
Is that possible for believers to have on earth?

Just as sanctification is a daily process
I believe that the perfection of faith is a daily one as well
Hebrews 12 says to look to Jesus, the perfecter of faith
In every trial, look to Jesus

Fear is a paralyzer
Fear keeps you silent
Fear keeps you still
But faith calls you higher

So I fix my eyes on You
Perfecter of my faith
I fix my eyes on You
Every single day

Every obstacle breeds an opportunity for growth
An opportunity for your faith to be perfected
An opportunity to look up and gaze upon Your Father
Oh weary one, consider Him

"We do this by keeping our eyes on Jesus, the champion who initiates
and perfects our faith. Because of the joy awaiting him, he endured the
cross, disregarding its shame. Now he is seated in the place of honor
beside God's throne."
Hebrews 12:2 NLT

The Sheep and the Shepherd (Psalms 23)

I awake and prepare for the day
It's not the unknown that makes me afraid
Not when I'm the canvas created Your way

Like a sheep I'll learn Your voice
Recognize Your face and see Your hand
There's no striving when I'm in Your will
Just grace and a law operated in love

I'm not blindly going into the wild when I'm following
Your voice
I'll turn upon a whisper
I'll leap upon a shout

I look on the past and know You've
Provided and guided in every field and season
Plucked from darkness
Gathered from harm
Saved from evil

If history proves true then I know You'll carry me through
So even when the sun fades
An eternal light will flame

I lie down in peace and retreat beside a cool stream
Refreshed by every word You speak
In awe that You know me

I realized today You have led me every step of the way
You're the Shepherd and I Your sheep
Attending to every word You speak

The Valley

He holds you when you're weak
He holds you when you're strong
When you feel like you have nothing to bring
or when you feel like you can conquer it all

Don't be surprised if in the lows you feel His peace even
more so
You feel His strength carrying you through each minute or
you hear His voice above most

In fact, expect it!
There's a blessing to it all and a mystery you might never
know

Humbling it is to admit to ourselves that only He can
deliver
redeem
and defend

I wrote this poem the evening my mom received a heartbreaking diagnosis. The cancer had entered her brain and Christmas was a week away. I remember feeling hopeful and expectant, knowing that God could touch her in an instant. But I texted her a portion of this poem to uplift her soul. She was a strong and faith-filled woman whose steadfast trust in the Lord has left such a legacy and imprint on so many people's lives. Whether you feel weak or strong in the moment, the ability to rest is in knowing that God holds your life and He reigns above it all - all sickness, cancer, and disease.

Shine

When all is dark and the path before me is unlit
Jesus, will You shine a little light, please?

When the sun has gone to sleep and the moon is slow to
wake
Jesus, will You shine a little light, please?

When winter has fully arrived and summer is yet a dream
Jesus, will You shine a little light, please?

When hope fades and feels like an arms length away
Jesus, will You shine a little light, please?

"Do not gloat over me, my enemies!
For though I fall, I will rise again.
Though I sit in darkness,
the Lord will be my light."
Micah 7:8 NLT

The Widow's Plea

I don't have much left to give
There's just a little oil left
I don't have much left to give
There's just a little flour left

God, can You even see me?
I'm barely hanging on
God, can You even hear?
I said I'm barely hanging on

And You said -
Lean into me, I am your covering
Press on - there is more - more than your eyes can see
I am your hope
I hold your peace
I am more than you've ever dreamed

I'm leaning into You, but I still have to make my move
So I go outside to collect what little I can find for food

I look across the field and see -
Is that an angel You've sent me?
I look across the field and see
Providence is beckoning

You say
Lean into me, I am your covering
Press on - there is more - more than your eyes can see
I am your hope
I hold your peace
I am more than you've ever dreamed

cont.

The sticks that you bring are enough for me
What little you have is still an offering
I can do more with a willing heart
I can do more than you ever thought

A song based on the story of Elijah and the Widow found in 1 Kings
17.

Still Praise

I'll praise through the pain
When I feel it returning
I better start declaring
That You're good
That You love me
And Your plans for me are full of hope

This short poem is simply a reminder that when we feel released worries, surrendered pain, and burdens we've laid upon the Lord return, it's important that we still praise. It's important that we still declare His goodness over our lives and situations. The truth of who God is does not change. He is still good. He is still love, and He loves you. His plans still speak of hope.

Joy Infused

When it's hard to worship
When it's hard to praise
Shout

When it's hard to laugh
When it's hard to smile
Sing

When it's hard to speak
When it's hard to think
Dance

For the joy of the Lord will
Shoot through your veins
And give you hope anew

Hope will be released
Spirit of fear to flee!

Then he said to them, "Go your way, eat the fat, drink the sweet, and
send portions to those for whom nothing is prepared;
for *this* day *is* holy to our Lord. Do not sorrow, for the joy of
the Lord is your strength."
Nehemiah 8:10 NKJV

A Season of Grace

Simple Trust

I don't know how good it can be
But here it is Lord, my offering
I trust You now

My cares and worries don't stand a chance
When they're placed in Your hands
I trust You now

Time has no fight with me
No more begging, this my plea
I trust You now

I am expectant
Won't You move?
I trust You now

"Cast all your anxiety on him because he cares for you."
1 Peter 5:7 NIV

Weak

How is there honor to be found in weakness
when I crave to be so strong?
I thirst for strength

Scripture claims it's an honor to be weak -
a privilege, even

Jesus has a way of transfiguring our natural thoughts

His Word, asking us to see from above
His Spirit, holding us to it
His Love, cradling us in it

The power of Christ in me
is made strong in my weakness

The proof is you can live content
The proof is you can live with joy
The proof is you can live in peace

There is honor in weakness
because my flesh glorifies Him even more so
when I am weak

But he said to me, "My grace is sufficient for you, for my power is
made perfect in weakness." Therefore I will boast all the more gladly
about my weaknesses, so that Christ's power may rest on me.
2 Corinthians 12:9 NIV

Remembrance

Remember what I've said to you in the hidden
When no one was around
It was just you and I

Taking Communion
Talking about everything in your life
Remember the secrets that I've shared

Oh do you remember?

Draw near and I'm here
Come closer
I've been waiting right here

I'm not far and I'm not in the distant
I'm more present than you know

Remember
Remember
Will you remember?

Like a whisper in the wind
Like a hug from a dear friend
Like guidance from a father
It's how I lead my children

Like a fire from within
Shepherding till then end
Holy Spirit lighting the way
It's how I lead my children

I'll go to where You're calling me to
Recalling Your ways even as a child
You're a friend forever

Oh Father -
I will look on my past
and remember

"Remember the days of old;
consider the generations long past.
Ask your father and he will tell you,
your elders, and they will explain to you."
Deuteronomy 32:7 NIV

Infilling

Walk a little further
Wait a little longer
A spring of living water
Is right around the corner

Get ready to drink deep
I've given you the thirst for it
The journey wasn't in vain
You were obedient all the way

The dryness is not the absence of my presence
The dryness is an indicator that you've not yet been fully satisfied
I ask my children to hunger and thirst after righteousness
My promise to you is that you will be filled!

As Christians we cannot be fooled that obedience to Jesus leads to immediate outcome. That's rarely the case! A step of faith is taken, and then plenty more steps of faith must follow. It's not a test, but it's all about relationship with the Father. It's a journey! When we hunger and thirst after one thing (Him) we will be satisfied. Mathew 6:33 says to seek first the kingdom of God and his righteousness, and all these things will be added to you.

Gold Mine

A piece of the masterpiece
You reveal to me in due time

A color
A symbol
A piece of Your mind

The splendor
The greatness
The beauty

You hold it all
It's a gold mine, really

"Splendor and majesty are before him; strength and glory are in his
sanctuary."
Psalm 96:6 NIV

My Best Friend

You go before me
You're already there
and yet still You walk with me
Showing off all Your wonders

You're walking beside me
Holding my hand
Closer than a brother and more than a friend
You live in me

I'll tell You my secrets
I'll tell You my plans
We'll laugh as we enter into the promised land

You don't let go
You won't let go
Because You know me
You are for me

"The LORD himself goes before you and will be with you; he will
never leave you nor forsake you. Do not be afraid; do not be
discouraged."
Deuteronomy 31:8 NIV

A Call to Live Surrendered

Simply being good is not good enough
Having a kind heart and a nice smile may get you far

But what gets you into eternity is a surrendered
And sanctified walk with Jesus

Anybody can be good
But who will be surrendered?

God doesn't want us to just be good
He wants us to be His

He doesn't want us to just know His name
He wants us to seek His face

He doesn't want to just make us better
He wants to free us

He doesn't want to just make us clean
He wants to make us a bride

"Let's rejoice and be glad and give the glory to Him, because the marriage of the Lamb has come, and His bride has prepared herself. It was given to her to clothe herself in fine linen, bright and clean; for the fine linen is the righteous acts of the saints."
Revelation 19:7-9 NASB

The Heart Cleanse Prayer

I want to do a swift cleanse in you
Re-train you in the truth of who I am
A refresh

Lord, I give You permission
to remove what's not of You
Any thought or belief I've adopted as truth
that's contrary to Your Word

Something in the physical that could take years
takes You a moment in the supernatural
I'm willing and I'm ready
Transfigure this heart once more

swift: **moving or capable of moving with great speed**. a swift
runner. : occurring suddenly or within a very short time. a swift
transition.

One evening at church the Lord said to my spirit that He wanted to do
a "swift cleanse in me." I love that He said the word swift because Holy
Spirit can move within a moment and correct years of hurt, lies, or
something we have adopted as truth. I had recently moved to Texas and
knew there were some things He wanted to sort out within my heart.
This poem is our response to His loving correction in our thinking and
ways. We must remain open and submissive to what He wants to do.

Hidden

Singleness is not a curse
See this burden as a gift
Do you feel Him draw you near?
Do you understand the blessing of it?

You feel you're hidden
What a safe place to be
Minding your business
Sowing your seeds

Though the grace of being alone is lifting
The desire to have a partner is only increasing
Jesus, let faith for that arise!
Faith expectations and not just preconceived notions

"Only, let each one live the life which the Lord has assigned him, and to
which God has called him [for each person is unique and is accountable
for his choices and conduct, let him walk in this way]. This is the rule I
make in all the churches."
1 Corinthians 7:17 AMP

Under His Canopy

A promise from God will never be broken
So you can just rest

The Father's love cannot be undone
So you can just rest

The peace that He brings can be used as a covering
So you can just rest

Under His Canopy is the safest place to be
For it holds life, freedom, and security

It's not used as an excuse to just get by or make do
But it's a protection and a force for kingdom-life moves

I hear Him say -

Come under my wing
for protection I bring
Are you tired?
Weary?
In need of strength?

Come under my wing
for you'll be restored
I'll carry you through it all
So you can just rest

I hold light
I hold time
And I hold the air

Good night
Sleep tight
Just rest

"He will cover you *and* completely protect you with His pinions,
And under His wings you will find refuge;
His faithfulness is a shield and a wall."
Psalm 91:4 AMP

Limited Love

I want to give you better, child

It's hard to trust that there's better
I desire the power to understand the depths of Your love
Help me to see and understand, Lord

I hear the word 'counterfeit' in my spirit

Counterfeit: made in imitation of something else with intent
to deceive;
something likely to be mistaken for something of higher
value

That was a taste of limited love
I want to give you something that's
deeper
richer
sweeter

Selah

His Word protects us. I remember where I was when I had this brief conversation with the Lord. He told me He wanted to give me better and it was hard to believe that "better" existed. I asked for His help to believe when the word 'counterfeit' appeared in my spirit. I googled the definition, wanting to truly understand.

What stuck out to me most is that a counterfeit of something can so easily be mistaken for the real thing. Without discernment and wisdom, the counterfeit is an easy choice. How are you to know the difference if you haven't experienced the real thing? In God's kindness, He made me aware and wanted to lead me to *the real thing*. He wants to do that for us all. Will we trust Him?

"My beloved ones, don't ever **limit your joy** or fail to rejoice in the wonderful experience of knowing our Lord Jesus! I don't mind repeating what I've already written you because it protects you —"
Philippians 3:1 TPT

Let Go

Do you trust me with the details?
Let go

I'm letting go and falling into love
I'm letting go and abiding in trust

There's power to choose -
I don't want to choose from a place of fear
I want to make a choice based on faith

For Jesus is kind
He's alive
He's great in mercy

My mom once told me "a decision made in fear is never a good one."
Since then, I've thought about that nugget of truth before making
some big decisions. It's given me space to pause and think before
moving forward in some things.

Examination

Search me and know me that I may know myself more
So that nothing is hidden from You or I
That I too may understand my motive, my intent, my heart
For it sways and pulls me in every which way

Search me to know me, and know me to lead me
To lead me to the rock that is higher than I
To lead me to depths that are deeper than I
To where I am made new and mirror the image of You

I let go of offense
I let go of anxious ways
I let go of man being my measuring rod
I just want to be closer

"Search me, O God, and know my heart; test me and know my anxious thoughts. Point out anything in me that offends you, and lead me along the path of everlasting life."
Psalm 139:23-24 NLT

Free Will

There's a gift to be found in the freedom of choice
You leave it up to me

There's constraint in dictatorship
and You're not an abuser of power
but the author of love

If everything were up to You
Would I know the pleasure of choice?
Would I know the sadness of disappointment?
Would I know the pressure, the liberation, or the discovery
of several options?

You desire me to be glad!

Knowing every good and perfect thing comes from above
You want me to have delight while on this earth
You grant me the freedom to choose You
All the while You would choose me, again and again

"Everything is permissible for me, but not all things are beneficial.
Everything is permissible for me, but I will not be enslaved by anything
[and brought under its power, allowing it to control me]."
1 Corinthians 6:12 AMP

This One Thing

Under the sun there's a season for everything
A lesson to be learned
A gift to be given

A time to laugh
A time to mourn
A time to dance
A time to sow
A time to reap
A time to rest

It all seems quite meaningless unless there's
one thing that remains

Did I love in the midst of it?
Did I love through the thick of it?
The days that seemed mundane and purposeless?

What did it teach me?
What did I learn?
Do I look more like my Savior or more like this world?

If I reflect Him even just a little more -
than the seasons where I felt
the most tested and worn
have just received their reward

"For everything there is a season, and a time for every matter under
heaven."
Ecclesiastes 3:1 ESV

Come to Me First

When I'm reminded of my shortcomings
Your love is there to fill my cup
Your grace is there to pick me up

I'm reminded of my position as a daughter
who is still growing, learning, and maturing
but one who has the full trust of her Father

You say to me -

Come here my child, and I'll pick up the pieces
Let my truth wash over you and you'll feel
the lies evaporate
You'll feel the shame leave

Come to me first
before all other comforts and lovers
Those who promise you ease and delight
They try to gain entry into your soul and a
foothold into your heart

Come to me child
and speak with me
face to face

I know it all but
I'm eager to hear it from you
I long to show you mercy and have
communion with the one I love

"For from his fullness we have all received, grace upon grace."
John 1:16 ESV

Higher

Your word alone can lift me
To a place that's higher than the mountains
I can see the shadows that they cast
I can see the earth below me

A daily routine of work and worry
Is there no rest for the weary?
A day where time will stand still with no rush or hurry?

Your hand is my covering
Your face reflects my hope
Your heart carries my security

Now that You've taken me higher,
I can see from Your perspective
A day to You holds endless possibilities
Moments for You to do the miraculous
For these moments are Your blinks of wonder

A poem written from the clouds (in an airplane).

Clarity

I have prioritized gaining clarity
I have made it the ultimate prize
I've traded the promise of
"I will be with you in deep waters"
for any clear picture I can create in my mind

But faith isn't simply having a belief in God -
it's having a deep trust that His will in my life
will be made complete

Nothing is beyond His repair
Nothing is beyond His redemptive work
Nothing is wasted

I can be too fearful to act or to step out -
What if my mistake is beyond reproach?

That is a lie

When you're swimming through murky water
you'll grasp for anything that looks clear

But in the midst of the unforeseen
choose to go in deep and cling to Jesus
He'll bring the peace
joy
and in time -
clarity

Emotions of the heart will either take you by storm
or guide you

Frustrate you
or reveal the insides of your heart

Our God is full of compassion
So peace can still be present in the unknown

Clarity is not the prize -
Christ is

A lesson on clarity. It comes with proximity, and even then, it
comes with trust.

A Life on the Altar

God, are You happy with me?
Are You pleased with my days?

Joy and satisfaction reside
in the hearts of those who live on the altar
Build your life there
Happy are those who dwell in my house

Those who live on the altar won't burn out
It's offering yourself to the Lord everyday
Your time
Your desires
Your plans

A willingness for your time to be interrupted
An allowance for a shuffled schedule
Seek Him first in the morning and all
the tasks, meetings, and errands will fall into place

Happy is He who makes time for the one
Happy is He who makes time for the Son

"The one thing I ask of the Lord—
the thing I seek most—
is to live in the house of the Lord all the days of my life,
delighting in the Lord's perfections
and meditating in his Temple."
Psalm 27:4 NLT

The Final Sabbath

Rest to run well
Rest to work well
until the coming of the Lord

Find the rhythm of work and rest
because there is
grace for the pace and
grace for the race

A day of sabbath is practice
for the grand finale!
Rest now to run hard until the Lord's
final sabbath!

Just as God rested on the seventh day from work
so we too shall rest
Lest we fall into disobedience and lend a foothold
to sin

Rest is a command
Rest is a gift
Rest is vital
Rest is an act of obedience

"So there is a special rest still waiting for the people of God."
Hebrews 4:9 NLT

He Is Everything

Child, what is it that you need from me?

Are you in need of comfort?
I am He.
Are you in need of acceptance?
I am He.
Are you in need of forgiveness?
I am He.
Are you in need of love?
I am He.
Are you in need of protection?
I am He.

Child, I could go on
You see
Whatever you need, you find in me
I am He who has redeemed you!
I am He who has set you free!
Whatever you're searching for
again I say, you will find in me

You search and search for meaning in earthly things
Trying to catch a glimpse of a light
Trying to find something "good"
in something that simply does not hold it

What is it you're searching for?
Allow me to be that for you
I am He

A Reminder to Rest

Oh to rest in His presence for the sake
of greater intimacy with Him
To say no to distractions
and to only pursue routes that take
me to greater depths in Him

To not strive and run for all the friendships
but trust that the Lord will place the people
in my path who are to be
in this season of my life

What's meant for me will not pass me by
I don't need to seek
I've come here
There they'll be

When God spoke to me about moving to Texas, I remember instantly
knowing there was a community of God fearing people that I would
"run the race" with. I thought how cool would it be if they were
expecting me. When I got there, everything was new and exciting! But
that still small voice was a comfort to me, reminding me of this group
of people, this community that I would settle into. There was no need
to strive to find what God had promised me.

Hour By Hour

I want a faith that's tried and true
To recognize Your hand in all that you do
Traces of Your goodness
Imprints of Your presence

In the good, I want to feel You there
In the hard, I want to know You're near
Oh God, come, find me faithful

Hour by hour
I'll choose hope over the fear
Hour by hour
Give me eyes to see the clear
Hour by hour
It's Your hand that leads me still
Hour by hour
Guide me into Your perfect will

I want an all-consuming peace
wrapped tight around me
A never-ending grace
One that sustains this rugged race

In the good, I want to feel You there
In the hard, I want to know You're near
Oh God, I'll choose to dwell here with You

This is what it means to have faith
To rest in not knowing every step of the way
This is what it means to have hope
A daily grace and a weighted soul

This is what it means to have trust
To know that You'll do what You say
I've counted the cost of a life with You
and You're worth the risk

"Moreover, it is required of stewards that they be found faithful."
1 Corinthians 4:2 ESV

Fruit

A prayer for the fruits of the Spirit to not just be virtues
but actions that exhibit themselves daily
I pray I have love for the most difficult being
May Yours abundantly overflow in the moment

I pray I have joy in the hardest of times
when I'm likely to grumble and complain
I pray for peace in the swirliest of storms
that I don't crumble under but rise above

I pray for patience the moment I want to scream
when my flesh tries to show itself in the ugliest form
I pray for kindness in the moments when it's least deserved
May it be authentic in tone and pure in motive

I pray for goodness to follow me all my days
but also to chase Your goodness when it's made visible to me
I pray for faithfulness in all my pursuits
and to finish what I start

I pray for a gentle and surrendered heart as my tongue speaks
slowly with a mind that's unassuming
I pray for spirit-strength
That Your lordship is the supreme authority in my life

Lord, give me the desire to release control!
Help me not to worry about trivial things that hold no weight
Mindless games that steal my peace and joy
Turning me into someone I don't want to be

Mercy

I called to You in a hurry
I called to You in worry
You answered me with mercy

I called to You in fear
I called to You in fury
You answered me with mercy

I called to You in deep waters
I called to You in miry depths
You answered me with mercy

I called to You in guilt
I called to You in shame
You answered me with mercy

I called to You in trouble
I called to You in fault
You answered me with mercy

"But God, being rich in mercy, because of the great love with which he
loved us, even when we were dead in our trespasses, made us alive
together with Christ—by grace you have been saved"—
Ephesians 2:4-5 ESV

A Season of Growth

Dig, Plant, Sow

Lord, I come to You again
If I plant the seeds, will You water them?
If I sow in darkness
If I dig in spite of not knowing what will grow
Will You be faithful to water?

Am I doubting that You'll complete Your side of the
bargain?
What more could You possibly owe me?

If You ask something of me
You surely know better

So I won't settle for good enough
I'll dig in deep
Take a risk and plant the seed
Hopefully expectant that the water is a guarantee

"I planted, Apollos watered, but God gave the growth."
1 Corinthians 3:6 ESV

Mustard Seed

I know You can
I know You care
My faith is there

Time goes by
And I know You can
I believe You still care

What I see in the physical is progressing
I know You see
I know You care

Breathe in
Breathe out
I know You're here

I have just a mustard seed left
But You say it's enough faith
To do wonders with

Matthew 17:20 NIV - He replied, "Because you have so little faith. Truly I tell you, if you have faith as small as a mustard seed, you can say to this mountain, 'Move from here to there,' and it will move. Nothing will be impossible for you."

The verse tells me that I can say to the mountain - be moved! And that nothing will be impossible. God has given us the authority to speak to things **according to the level of our faith.** So when I see things in the physical that don't make sense or don't add up, I have to ask myself, "have I put my faith into practice?" Have I done what the scriptures ask of me according to my level of faith and tell the mountain to move? I remind myself of what God says is possible. I let that take me farther than my current feelings, because His Word will always outrun them.

Movement

There's an unrest in my bones
An unsettling in my soul
A hunger for the new
A longing to see You move

In this world but not of it -
Have we mirrored living like our neighbor too closely?
Made it to be an extravagant thing?
Has it cost us contentment?

Someone wise once said
Always set your life up for change
Position your heart for such
Because where the Spirit moves, you go

So I have found home in Your love
And pitched my tent in Your dwelling
Always expectant in Your presence
Remaining hopeful, even in the mundane

"If you try to hang on to your life, you will lose it. But if you give up
your life for my sake, you will save it."
Matthew 16:25 NLT

Soar

Maybe I'll fall
With every good idea and dream I've dreamt
Falling with me, fast
It's quite the risk
What's the cost?
I could really fall
Hard

Maybe I'll fly
With every good idea and dream I've dreamt
Flying with me, fast
It's quite the risk
What's the cost?
I could really fly
High

What's your gut telling?
What's your heart saying?
Faith over logic -
Can they be one of the same?
Sometimes you must count the cost
No matter the risk
Because maybe, just maybe
You'll soar

…"for we walk by faith, not by sight [living our lives in a manner
consistent with our confident belief in God's promises]"—
2 Corinthians 5:7 AMP

Whispers

In a noisy and crazed world
I want to speak to you in whispers
I can use signs and wonders to show you my glory
But often it's for those whose eyes have been uncovered
and whose hearts have been enlightened

For those who have wonder like a child -
It's those that the kingdom of heaven becomes tangible to
They don't have to wait until heaven but they can experience
it now
Those that have not hardened their hearts to the world,
 religion, and disappointment

I'll show you how to keep your heart tender and pure
I'll teach you how to have joy even when your mind feels at
war
Speak to your thoughts and emotions to come into alignment
with my Word and truth
For the language of heaven is love

The Lord said, "Go out and stand on the mountain in the presence of
the Lord, for the Lord is about to pass by." Then a great and powerful
wind tore the mountains apart and shattered the rocks before the Lord,
but the Lord was not in the wind. After the wind there was an
earthquake, but the Lord was not in the earthquake. After the
earthquake came a fire, but the Lord was not in the fire. And after the
fire came a gentle whisper.
1 Kings 19:11-12 NIV

Harvest

In some seasons we sow, others we reap
We dig, plant, and wait for something great to appear
Unsure of the outcome but we have a slight clue

It's the time between the sow and the reap
That's the hardest for me
Not knowing how long it will last

Yet I remain hopeful because I know how this ends
A bountiful harvest to enjoy once again
And then one morning, you know something's changed
You feel it in the air

It's time

With a praise on my lips and a dance in my soul
I thank Jesus for this wonderful gift He bestowed

That is what I love about a new season -
The hopefulness it yields
A new song I start to sing
A fresh zeal for life it brings

"Let us not become weary in doing good, for at the proper time we will
reap a harvest if we do not give up."
Galatians 6:9 NIV

Pursuit

What offense can be turned into intercession?
What offense can be turned into prayer?
What offense can be turned into a hunger for more?

I've tasted and I've seen
And now it's time to grow
The milk no longer satisfies
The time of drinking this staple over and over was good
But -
It's time for more
It's time to add
It's time to multiply

It's all apart of Your design
A foundation for babies and for believers
You've placed in us a hunger for more

When something is new
There is question and curiosity
And that's okay
It's not something to run from
But dig into and ask questions

You'll show
You'll reveal
I'll trust You - Holy Spirit
Revealer of truth and light

Come, Church -
Let's continue to pursue and persist

The Better Thing

Your presence is the promise
One You freely give
Your face is the gift
I'll behold all my days

I'll choose the better thing
Pausing and sitting still before You
All the other tasks can wait
You are my priority

Help me to quiet my soul and silence the noise
I want to give You the reverence You deserve
With no other obligation
You have my full attention

"I heard your voice in my heart say, "Come, seek my face;" my inner
being responded, "Yahweh, I'm seeking your face with all my heart."
Psalms 27:8 TPT

Wineskins

Do not place new wine into an old wineskin
Do not fit an old dream into a new season
Steward what the Lord is calling you to now
Unafraid to step into the unknown

The previous season had its purpose and served its cause
But what takes you into the future is fresh perspective
A renewed sense of calling and a rhema word

Walk out this new season with daily obedience
so that the calling and season are both savored and
persevered

If you feel you missed it
If you feel you disobeyed
He'll kindly re-route you and show you the way

Don't pity yourself for the choices you've made
Don't shame yourself into thinking this isn't God's way

Years ago I applied for a job that I was so excited about! The job posting was delayed for about a year, and I waited and waited to receive a call for an interview. The day came when I received the call. As I was waiting to be called in for the interview, I began to feel sick to my stomach and immediately felt like I shouldn't be there. I prayed and asked God why I was feeling that way and He spoke, "Do not put new wine into an old wineskin." Up until that point I hadn't realized that's what I was doing. A year had gone by and I hadn't checked in with God to see if that's what He had for me. Had I chosen to accept the position and ignore that still small voice, who knows where disobedience would have led me.

Confession

Our hearts weren't meant to hold secrets
Captivated by the hush noises and whispers
Confession to one another was a daily practice of the early
Church
Confessing to one another and sharing our burdens

Praying for one another so that healing may come
Where two or more are gathered, our great high priest,
brother, and friend is present
Holy Spirit, search our hearts yet again
Because we can't heal what we don't feel

Equip us by Your Spirit to forgive
Equip us by Your Spirit to heal
You don't reject a broken and repentant heart
Restoration can now begin

"Many of those who believed now came and openly confessed what
they had done."
Acts 19:18 NIV

The Glory of Light

Show me Your love
Show me Your heart
Lift the veil
Flame the spark

Spirit of wisdom and revelation
Make Yourself known
The glory of Your light
To be shown

This little light of mine is not very little
You created it to be immaculate
Bright and grand for all to take notice
It cannot be hidden

One day
Daylight will cease to exist
What will guide us?
Who will be our eyes?

The Lamb will be our light
His glory is bright enough

A King has come
And a King shall reign
Let heaven and nature sing

"And the city has no need of sun or moon to shine on it, for the glory
of God gives it light, and its lamp is the Lamb."
Revelation 21:23 ESV

Reconnect

The Lord is speaking to those who turn
an ear towards heaven
To those who desire to see His hand move among the earth
To those who seek Him with pure hearts
To those who cling to His wisdom and wear it like a necklace

We don't see what God sees
We don't know what God knows
We don't have His insight and understanding
Therefore, we must ask for it!

Ask for His kingdom reality
Ask for heaven's perspective
Ask Holy Spirit to set our minds on things above
Ask and receive

"And your ears shall hear a word behind you, saying, "This is the way,
walk in it," when you turn to the right or when you turn to the left."
Isaiah 30:21 ESV

Bloom and Grow

A little water and light is all you need
A shift in the ground, a change in the weather
Blossom and grow may you bloom and grow
Bloom and grow forever

Your roots will prevail
Your foundation will withstand
Blossom and grow may you bloom and grow
Bloom and grow forever

When gusts of wind blow
And cracks of drought break through
Blossom and grow may you bloom and grow
Bloom and grow forever

My mom used to sing me a lullaby she made up to the melody of
Edelweiss from the Sound of Music. She'd sing "I love you; You love
me. Bless my Katelyn forever. Blossom and grow may you bloom and
grow, bloom and grow forever. I love you; You love me. Bless my
Katelyn forever." I turned it into a poem but when I hear the phrase
"bloom and grow," I can't help but think of that melody and know
those words best belong in that sweet lullaby.

An Audience of One

What you've sown in secret
you will see bloom
If you don't see it right away
wait for it

If only your eyes ever see it -
will that be enough for you?

A whispered promise in your ear
meant only for your heart to know and for your eyes to see -
would you still testify to God's greatness
and faithfulness?

Who are you entertaining?
Who is in your audience?
Who are you looking to hear a clap from?

Your standing ovation awaits in heaven
and even then you'll be bowing at His feet

May Jesus be the only one you ever dare to please

"And whenever the living creatures give glory and honor and thanks to
him who is seated on the throne, who lives forever and ever, the
twenty-four elders fall down before him who is seated on the throne
and worship him who lives forever and ever. They cast their crowns
before the throne, saying,

"Worthy are you, our Lord and God,
to receive glory and honor and power,
for you created all things,
and by your will they existed and were created."
Revelation 4:9-11 ESV

Usher

If you're struggling to hear the voice of God
If you're eager to understand His ways and
discern His will for your life -
You don't have to look far

He speaks to us by His son
He speaks to us through His creation
He speaks to us by communicating as you
would to a brother, father, or friend

His words are guiding truth that doesn't change
His promises are lifetime guarantees
His presence is easy to enter into
Say His name and welcome Him in

"Long ago, at many times and in many ways, God spoke to our fathers
by the prophets, but in these last days he has spoken to us by his Son,
whom he appointed the heir of all things, through whom also he
created the world."
Hebrews 1:1-2 ESV

Obedience

I've come to the conclusion that no matter what You ask
My answer is Yes
It's scary but it's worth it

When we ask You to move
When we desire revival
When we long for change
We better be ready to do what You say

My mind is made up
I'm choosing obedience
Whatever the cost is
Holy Spirit, help my spirit-man not lag

"Do not merely listen to the word, and so deceive yourselves. Do what
it says."
James 1:22 NIV

Yes

I'll keep saying yes to You
No matter the cost
Whatever the risk

May my obedience be like a love song
A pleasing fragrance that rises from my heart to the heavens
If a road in life takes me where I've not imagined -
Who can know Your plans?

I'll let faith drive and Your voice be the guide
I'll keep saying yes to You even when others don't
understand
There may be an easier way but You've not called me into
complacency
The thought of staying the same is unsettling

I'm learning more and more that we only have one life to
live
One life to make an impact for Your cause

I used to believe it had little to do with me
But now I see my yes is all encompassing

Every day of my life
I wake up to answer the question
"Will you follow me?"

He roams the earth
waiting and listening for where the "yes" will echo from
With eyes on His beloved
He wonders if the yes will come from you

Individualism vs. Collectivism

On your own -
The thought at first is thrilling
But then a sad realization washes over
and it's chilling
Because truth be told
Individualism is a lonely road

It becomes a path to isolation
If communion was the original plan
Then anything opposite of that is a means to an end

With people -
There is gain
An abundance of the things we lack
Our flesh wants to fight it
To provide in our own strength
But alone -
We simply cannot

There is freedom in submitting
There is joy in fellowship
There is life to be lived
Together

"They were continually *and* faithfully devoting themselves to the
instruction of the apostles, and to fellowship, to eating meals together
and to prayers."
Acts 2:42 AMP

Arise

Arise you weary sleeper and stand
Wear wisdom like a necklace
Find friendship with time
Daily give thanks to God

Arise you weary sleeper and dance
Don't be fooled by empty words
But seek the things above
Your strength will be renewed

Arise you weary sleeper and sing
Sing of sweet melodies
And watch your foes flee
For those who hear will live

Arise you weary sleeper and fight
For the light is on your side
All that is good, right, and true
You can now see

For this reason it says,
"Awake, sleeper,
And arise from the dead,
And Christ will shine on you."
Ephesians 5:14 NASB

Prune

This deep work of pruning - isn't it lovely?
This deep work of pruning - isn't it refining?
Might as well throw me into fire!

This deep work of pruning -
the stripping of anything that clings
It's the bruising, the scarring, the story of in between
This deep work of pruning - all for what?
So that the old man can die?

No
So old can be reborn
So old can go farther, live longer, and run faster
So old can dream bigger, grow wiser, reach wider

There's nothing wrong with old
Pruning comes with age
The etching comes with time
There is beauty in a full life that was not rushed
by earthly compromise

The young can go through pruning, too
Get ready for the same demise
Rest assured this deep work He's doing
won't be sown in vain

Submit to the pruning so that His love
may be tested and purified within
Repurposed for its original plan

I submit though I wonder -

cont.

What lives on the other side?
Heavens awaits to answer

"Every branch in Me that does not bear fruit, He takes away; and every branch that continues to bear fruit, He [repeatedly] prunes, so that it will bear more fruit [even richer and finer fruit]."
John 15:2 AMP

What Is Truth?

I don't want to grab at anything just because it's something
because conformity is not unity
Collective agreement on something does not make it true
if contrary to Your Word

I don't want to be tossed by the waves or
entertained by the sway of the wind
Calling out for Your name
but not seeking Your face

I desire a faith that speaks
An understanding and depth of Your grace
A long history of knowing Your love and loving You in
return
A collection of sacred moments of worship before You
A steadfast union rooted in joy unspeakable and hope
abounding

Cultural opinions and foolish ideologies ring out like a
sounding gong
It screams of offense to Your name
No, I won't grab at anything just because it's something
I'll let Your truth be the guide

"However, when He, the Spirit of truth, has come, He will guide you
into all truth; for He will not speak on His own *authority,* but whatever
He hears He will speak; and He will tell you things to come."
John 16:13 NKJV

Capacity

To be used to my fullest capacity
I remind myself that movement starts with me

When I move, I'll see You move
If I'm willing, there You"ll be

But what if I can't contain all that You want me to hold?

What if that's the point of surrender?
What if that's the purpose of grace?

To flourish, it requires a yielding
A movement that is resolved yet steady

Trust grows deeper when my will is surrendered

To be dependent on Christ is not a weak thing
To be a co-laborer with Him is no small task

"I am the vine, you *are* the branches. He who abides in Me, and I in
him, bears much fruit; for without Me you can do nothing."
John 15:5 NKJV

Begin

You see
You perceive
You understand

You do with what I give you and watch it grow
Higher and higher with the roots spreading deeper

Stronger and stronger
Your faith is increasing

The plan is outlined in my hand
You don't need a map to comprehend

A willing heart and opened mind will do just fine
It's time to begin

"But blessed [spiritually aware, and favored by God] are your eyes,
because they see; and your ears, because they hear. I assure
you *and* most solemnly say to you, many prophets and righteous
men [who were honorable and in right standing with God] longed to
see what you see, and did not see it, and to hear what you hear, and did
not hear it."
Matthew 13:16-18 AMP

Limitless

I'm not full until I have all of You
There's a longing in my heart for heaven
For heaven has no limits
because you're a limitless God

Abundance has no markers
Abundance has no fences
It's a wide open space

But I can have as much of You as I want
All of You is more than enough
and if it's full access that I crave then guess what?
I have it!

I don't live in scarcity
I don't live like You can't do the impossible
I don't live like You're unsure of what tomorrow holds
I don't live like one who doesn't serve an all knowing and all
consuming God

I live in abundance
I live a full life
I live a good life
I live in a supernatural reality where I live like You exist

Because guess what?
You do!

I'm satisfied because You're here
But I live for the more
Always for the more

C. S. Lewis wrote, "If I find in myself desires which nothing in this world can satisfy, the only logical explanation is that I was made for another world."

God wants us to hunger and thirst for Him and to never be satisfied. He desires for us to seek Him all our days. There's a longing in us as believers to crave and desire the things of Heaven. That longing to be "home" was placed in us the moment we received the breath of life. God makes His home in us on earth, but one day we will make our home with Him in Heaven. {Paul understood this - Philippians 1:22-24}

The Answered Door

I'm desperate to hear from You
I'm desperate to know You more

One word and I'm satisfied
Your love, forever glorified
One taste of Your goodness
I'll never hunger again

Your gaze -
I'm locked in

I've searched in faith that You'd appear
I've knocked in expectation that You'd answer
When out You came, why was I surprised?
Deep down I knew You would

So now with confidence I come
I think I'll knock just once this time
But when I arrived, the door was opened wide
Out You came and said - "Child, why so surprised?"

So now with laughter I come
For nothing is hidden from You!
You're closer than the air I breathe
Speak Your name and all fear rolls away

Hand in hand I'll walk down this road with You
Sharing all of my stories as if You never knew
That's the joy in having a relationship with You
There's no fear and shame in the unseen

For You know all
And yet You still love me

"Ask *and* keep on asking and it will be given to you; seek *and* keep on
seeking and you will find; knock *and* keep on knocking and the door
will be opened to you."
Matthew 7:7 AMP

Pause

Stop whatever you're doing and find Jesus
Pause -
without the pressure of time and know Him
Look around and see Him

Will you notice Him in nature -
in the budding of a flower
the fall of spring rain
or even in the boring and mundane?

Will you hear Him in the melody of a symphony -
in the sounds of your own family
the hush of an early morning
or the fading of an evening?

Stop whatever you're doing and find Jesus
The more you seek, the more you'll find
The more you find, the more you'll learn
that His Spirit loves to dwell in the midst of His children

Look -
and find Him everywhere

"For since the creation of the world God's invisible qualities—his
eternal power and divine nature—have been clearly seen, being
understood from what has been made, so that people are without
excuse."
Romans 1:20 NIV

"Lord, how wonderfully you bless the righteous. Your favor wraps around each one and covers them under your canopy of kindness and joy."
- Psalms 5:12 TPT

ABOUT THE AUTHOR

Katelyn Gannon lives in Columbus, OH with her husband and newborn son. She currently writes for a pro-life organization. Under the Canopy is her first book. Her writings have been featured in Darling Magazine, Be Still Magazine, Hosanna Revival, Grit & Virtue, and Propel Women. Furthermore, she loves writing songs for the Church. Katelyn desires to see people experience the true love of Christ and to see the Church live boldly and unashamed. In all her writings, she prays that the reader's heart would be reconnected to the Father.

To stay in touch with Katelyn, follow her @underthecanopyonline.

For book inquiries please email katelynmgannon@gmail.com.